The Fox

By Liza Charlesworth

ISBN: 978-1-339-02684-8

Art Director: Tannaz Fassihi; Designer: Tanya Chernyak
Photos ©: p7: Richard Seeley/Shutterstock.com. All other photos © Getty Images.

3 4 5 6 7 8 9 10   68   32 31 30 29 28 27 26 25 24

Printed in Jiaxing, China. First printing, August 2023.

■SCHOLASTIC

This red fox is a mom.
She has a set of fox kits!

Will the kits rest in the den?
No! A den is not fun.

But a pond is lots of fun.
The kits dip and sip.

The kits sit in the grass.
They yip and yell.

The kits jump in mud.

The kits run and skip.

They tug on a stick.

They nip and hug.

Sit, sip, yip, yell!
Run, skip, tug, hug!
At last, the fox kits nap.